May Gibbs Country CRAFT

Project Coordinator Nerée Hartog
Project designs by Lorell McIntyre & Janet Klepatzki
Photography by Andrew Elton
Styling by Louise Owens

BayBooks

An imprint of HarperCollins*Publishers*

Contents

Introduction

May Gibbs was born Cecilia May Gibbs in Surrey, England in 1877. In 1881 she emigrated to Australia with her parents and brothers. As a child she was actively encouraged by her parents to draw. Her first book, *Snugglepot and Cuddlepie*, was published in 1918 and has never been out of print. May went on to create more wonderful stories and characters which have entertained children and adults alike ever since.

Still Australia's most well-loved children's author and illustrator, her friendly bush creatures and adorable flower babies have delighted generations of Australian children. Her drawings and designs have become popular icons of Australian culture and remain a symbol of the beauty and fragility of the Australian bush.

Copyright of all May Gibbs' work rests with the Spastic Centre of New South Wales and the New South Wales Society for Children and Young Adults with Physical Disabilities and royalties from the sale of this book benefit these two charities. These beautiful projects inspired by May Gibbs' illustrations and stories are intended for personal use and not for any commercial purpose. They have been designed with the approval and co-operation of the copyright holders and their agent, Curtis Brown (Australia) Pty Ltd.

Découpage

Basic materials

These materials are used in each of the découpage projects in this book, in addition to the materials listed under each specific project.

FolkArt All Purpose Spray
Fine wet and dry sandpaper
Fine-tipped manicure or découpage scissors
Blu-Tack
Mod Podge
Soft brush
Brayer or small roller
Small sponge
Chux cloth
Tack rag (a lint-free cloth, moistened with a few
    drops of linseed oil)
FolkArt Satin Finish Waterbase Varnish
Good quality furniture wax
Soft cloth
Steel wool (size 0000)

Preparing the papers

Before cutting any papers, it is a good idea to seal them by spraying lightly and evenly with All Purpose Spray. To do this, spread out the sheet of paper and spray one side, allow it a few minutes to dry, then turn it over and spray the other side. This will protect the paper from colour bleed when it is wet and moist from the glue.

Cutting

Use very fine, sharp manicure scissors with a curved blade for best results with cutting. Hold the scissors with the curved blade turned out from the paper that is being cut. Try to feed the paper through the scissors and use the fine points to snip into tiny curves. Leave bridges between very fine stems.

Arranging a design

When considering the design for your découpage, it is important to take into consideration the use that the piece will be put to in the future. For example, the candlesticks will be seen from a number of angles at one time, while the tray and the fruit platter will both be used to hold other things in the centre, so decoration is best on the outside edge. It may be necessary to cut the design elements and arrange the selected pieces on the project before gluing, so that your own design can be built up and you can decide if the design is appropriate. It is often helpful to secure pieces with Blu-Tack and re-arrange them as required.

Once you have chosen the design, the gluing process can begin.

Applying the glue

When gluing in découpage always apply the glue to the hard surface, applying the Mod Podge quite liberally with a brush. Then place the cutout on top of the glue, laying it down as smoothly as possible so that you avoid trapping air underneath. Apply a coat of Mod Podge to the top of the cutout. Press down firmly with your fingers and squeeze any excess glue or air from underneath the paper, so that no ridges or air pockets remain.

It may be helpful to use a brayer or a small roller to assist with this step. Wipe away any excess glue with a damp chux cloth. It is important to allow each layer of paper to dry thoroughly before adding the next overlapping piece on top.

Repeat this procedure until the project is decorated as desired.

Applying the build-up layers

Next, begin to apply the build-up coats of Mod Podge, which will make the découpage papers merge into a smooth surface. Brush on at least 5 coats of Mod Podge, allowing each coat to completely dry for a minimum of 20 minutes between coats. Alternate direction and record on a scrap of paper to avoid a build up in one direction only. Wipe the project with a tack rag between each coat of Mod Podge to avoid lint.

When the 5 coats are completely dry it is possible to wet sand very, very lightly with fine wet and dry sandpaper. Although sanding is not normally carried out with less than 20 coats of varnish, it is possible when using Mod Podge because of the thick nature of this product, if extreme care is taken. If you are heavy-handed or in doubt, omit sanding until much later in the process. If you do decide to proceed with sanding, be sure to use the finest wet and dry paper available and work with plenty of water so that a good slurry provides a cushion between the paper and the project. Remove any sludge with a clean damp cloth, then allow the whole project to dry.

Next, apply another 5 coats of Mod Podge, again allowing to dry thoroughly between coats before repeating the sanding process. Don't forget to remove any residue and dry.

Varnishing

By now there should be 10 coats of Mod Podge so the varnishing can begin. Never add waterbased varnish to a project on a dull, humid or rainy day as waterbased varnish can cloud and this would ruin the whole project. It is better to be patient and produce a pleasing result after all the work you have done to bring the piece to this stage. FolkArt Waterbase Varnish has been used on the projects throughout this book. Again, it is essential to allow the project to dry thoroughly, for at least half an hour, between coats and to wipe with a tack rag to remove any dust. Record the direction of each coat applied until the paper seems to merge into a smooth surface. At least 20 coats of varnish are normally required.

Finishing

When the work has a smooth glass-like surface, the piece may be finished with a coat of wax. Use a good quality furniture wax. Warm the wax in a microwave oven for about 50 seconds (not in the tin) and have a cup of very hot water ready. Dip a soft lint-free cloth into the hot water, then into the wax. Rub the wax thickly over the project. Next, use 0000 steel wool to work the wax into the surface, rubbing with a light circular motion and always maintaining a good film of wax between the surface of the project and the steel wool.

Allow the wax coat to dry, then buff vigorously with a soft cloth.

Stencilling

Basic materials

These materials are used in each of the stencilling projects in this book, in addition to the materials listed under each specific project.

Acetate film for cutting stencil,
  such as Mylar Film or Simply Stencil film
Fine-tipped marker pen
Cutting mat
Scalpel or craft knife
Scotch Magic Tape
Turpentine
Paper towel
Palette, if using paint rather than crayons
Ruler

Tracing the design

Place acetate film over stencil design and trace, using a fine-tipped marker pen. Remember that a separate stencil will be required for each colour in the design. For example, the Bush Babies Place Mat on page 31 has a separate stencil for A) green leaves and hat, B) yellow leaves and hair, C) stems and D) babies, a total of four separate stencils which make up the design. Because of the number of different stencils required, it is essential that each sheet is labelled. In order that each sheet line up accurately with the others, to produce a coordinated picture, it is also essential to copy from the design the grid lines which are drawn in dots. Positioning these on the area to be stencilled will ensure that the project is straight, correct vertically and horizontally. It is also important to make sure that you have left enough space for a border around the outside edge of the film, so that you don't have a problem with the stencil brush slipping off the stencil as you work.

Cutting the sheet

When each section of the stencil has been traced onto its own sheet you are ready to begin cutting. Using a very sharp scapel or craft knife and a cutting mat, begin by piercing the film with the tip of the blade, then pulling gently but firmly towards yourself, following the traced line exactly. When there are curves or corners to follow move the film as well as the blade. Take care, when cutting tight curves or matching up to v-joints, not to over cut. If you slip and cut too far, a repair can be made with Scotch Magic Tape or masking tape applied to both sides of the sheet. Then cut over the repair again as though it was the original sheet. The cuts should be smooth and clean without ragged edges. When you have finished cutting, hold the stencil up to the light and check your work. If you are inexperienced, be critical of your work and aim to correct any errors as you gain experience.

Practice piece

Before applying the paint, practise on a piece of scrap paper. Check that the design is lined up correctly and that it is straight, check the spacing between each design. This is important, as you may need to 'squeeze and stretch', that is, leave just a little more space than on the original or just a little less space so that the design exactly fits the space you have. The 'squeezing and stretching' should be done in the middle part of the work and not left until the ends where it will be noticeable. Take note of this and use the rough copy to place against the area you are planning to work on, be it a wall, place mat or a cushion. It is also important to check the colours that you intend to use if you make changes from those listed in the book.

Applying the paint

Hold stencil in place on project with Scotch Magic Tape at the corners. Ideally, a different brush should be used for each colour on the stencil. If this is not possible, the brushes should be thoroughly cleaned and allowed to dry before progressing to the next colour.

Two types of paint have been used in this book:

1 ARTIST PAINT CRAYONS: These are oil-based paint in a stick form made especially for stencillers working on walls or surfaces that will be protected by varnish. Once cured, these paints can be wiped over with a damp cloth for cleaning. They are easy and economical to use as each crayon goes a very long way.

To use, simply scrape back a little of the self sealing covering to expose the moist crayon surface, then rub a circular patch of colour onto a corner of the stencil film. Next, take the stencil brush and gently rub it over the colour so that paint is picked up on the brush. Rub the brush in a circle on another part of the film to remove any excess. Now, moving your hand in a figure eight motion, rub the brush over the cut area of stencil with very light pressure to set in an edge of colour. Next, work in tight little circles going clockwise then anticlockwise over the area to be covered, until the desired depth of colour is reached.

If you wish to add shading of another or deeper colour, repeat the process in the area where you want the colour to be, for example, the leaves on the Bush Babies Place Mats on page 31 are stencilled in Wild Ivy Green, but a blue shading has been added to some by brushing on a little Ship's Fleet Navy, then adding a highlight to the tips of some leaves by brushing on Ol' Pioneer Red. The paint work should have a deeper colour around the edges and be paler in the centres.

2 FOLKART ACRYLIC COLOUR: This has been mixed with FolkArt Textile Medium 2:1, that is, 2 parts paint to 1 part textile medium and has been used on the fabrics for a permanent and washable finish.

The fabric paint is applied in two ways:
1 Pick up paint on the stencil brush but remove most of it onto a piece of paper towel before brushing onto the stencil. Brush with light even strokes from the outside towards the centre of the space, so that the colour is darker around the edge of the stencil with paler colour in the middle. This looks similar to the wall stencilling and is especially nice on light fabrics.

2 An opaque coloured look can also be achieved by brushing even colour over the whole area to be stencilled. Again, load the brush in the paint mixed with fabric medium and remove excess paint onto a piece of paper towel before working on the stencil. Begin at the outer edge, brushing in towards the centre. This sets in the edge and helps to prevent a ragged look. Then brush even colour over the remainder of the stencil, ensuring that the depth of colour is maintained throughout. This is more suited to medium to heavier fabrics and has been used for a country look on the apron and calico cushion.

Cleaning the stencils and brushes

After using the stencil, wipe away any residue of paint with a soft cloth and if necessary, wipe over with a cloth moistened with turps. Brushes can also be washed in turps. It may be a good idea to keep some turps in a small screw top jar with a kitchen scourer pad inside. To clean the brush, stroke over the turps-covered pad, then stroke the brush on paper towel or an old cloth until the brush is clean.

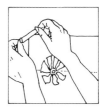

Tape stencil to surface that is to be worked on.

Remove protective self-seal from crayons.

Apply crayon to uncut part of stencil away from cutout area.

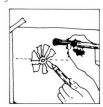

Use a brush to pick up paint and colour in cutout area.

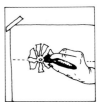

Highlight and shade area as desired.

To clean brushes: rub cleaner into bristles and rinse under warm water.

Folk Art

Basic materials

These materials are used in each of the folk art projects in this book, in addition to the materials listed under each specific project.

Sponge brush (for basecoat and varnish)
FolkArt All Purpose Spray
Tracing paper
Fine-tipped marker pen
Transfer paper (dark or light colour, depending on the base colour of project)
Stylus
Kneadable rubber
Palette (a large dinner plate, or commercial palette)
FolkArt Extender (to slow drying time of paint)
Water jar
FolkArt Satin Finish Waterbase Varnish
Fine sandpaper
Tack rag (a lint-free cloth, moistened with a few drops of linseed oil)

Basecoat

Most pieces require 2 or 3 basecoats to cover evenly, before design is transferred. This is applied with a sponge brush, allowing to dry and sanding lightly, between coats. Sometimes special finishes, such as sponging or scumbling, add interest to a background, and the basecoated surface is sprayed with FolkArt All Purpose Spray, either before or after this is done, depending on the specific project.

Transferring the design

The designs may be traced from the book onto tracing paper with a fine-tipped marker pen, or photocopied. Now place the chalk side of the transfer paper onto the basecoated surface of piece to be painted and tape it down. Then place the pattern, either traced or photocopied, on top of the transfer paper, centering the design, and tape it down. Using a stylus, gently trace over the pattern lines, checking to see if the lines are being transferred to your project. Do not apply too much pressure, especially on wood, as the lines will indent the timber.

Test a small area before drawing the whole design. The lines can be erased with a kneadable rubber and, at the completion of each project, it is necessary to check that no transfer lines are visible before the varnish is brushed on.

Finishing

Usually, 2 or 3 coats of waterbase varnish will protect the project well. Allow to dry between coats and sand lightly. Varnish should be applied with a ¾ glaze brush.

Brushes

In most projects, 3 brushes have been used. These are No. 3 Round, No. 8 Flat and No. 00 Liner. You should use whichever brush feels the most appropriate to the size of the area to be painted, although specific suggestions have been made in most places.

Painting techniques

Basing in

This is the first colour to be applied to the design. Moisten flat brush in water, blot on a cloth, then pick up some Extender. Blend brush back and forwards to work Extender into fibres. Load brush by picking up some colour and then working it into fibres, as described for Extender. Do not overload brush as this will produce thick ridges of paint. Blend by stroking brush on palette and build up several light coats of paint rather than one thick coat.

Floating and shading

Load brush with water and/or Extender. Dip one corner of brush into paint so that you pick up a triangle of colour. Stroke brush in one direction on palette, so that paint gradually blends from coloured edge to fade away across brush to clear Extender on the other side. This will allow you to add shading colour that automatically blends into the base colour. If colour flows right across brush, rinse and begin again. Blend each time you pick up more colour. When painting your project, place the side of the brush with the deepest colour against the area you want to be the darkest.

Highlighting

Highlighted areas receive more light and therefore appear to be a lighter shade than the base colour and shading. Float highlight colour onto base colour, as indicated in specific project.

Comma stroke

It is always advisable to practise first on white paper. With the brush loaded, rest your hand on the surface of the paper, touch the brush to the surface, push down on the brush to fan out the bristles, release the pressure and slowly pull the brush down, lifting it at the same time so that you watch the bristles gradually return to a fine point. Take your time with this brushstroke, as it needs a little control to achieve the fine point at the end of the stroke.

'S' stroke

Load the brush with paint, touch the brush to the surface, starting with a very fine line; slowly add pressure and at the same time, form an 'S' shape, then slowly release the pressure to allow the bristles to return to a fine point at the end of the stroke. A reverse 'S' shape is done the same way.

Side or single-loading the flat brush

Place a puddle of paint on your palette. Gently pull one side of your brush through the side of the puddle. Blend the colour by stroking the brush on a clean section of your palette until you can see the colour blending to the centre of your brush's fibres.

Brush mix

This is when paint is mixed with the brush giving an imperfect blend of the colours i.e. some of each colour can still be seen as the mix is not uniform. (Usually paint is mixed with a palette knife to give a perfect blend of the two or more colours to create a different colour.)

Loading the flat brush

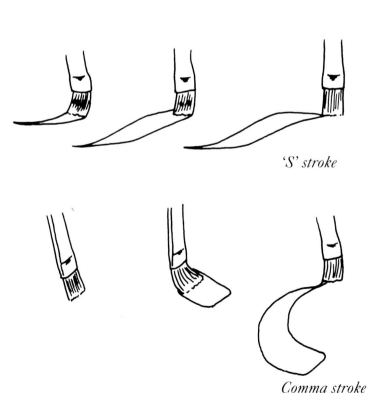

'S' stroke

Comma stroke

Among the Gum Trees

Bushland Bread Board

Classic Gumnut Babies, so loved by generations of Australian children, adorn a simple, country-style bread board.

Materials

As listed under Folk Art Basic Materials, on page 12.

BASE COLOUR:
FolkArt Acrylic Colour: Green Meadow

PAINT:
FolkArt Acrylic Colours: Licorice, Almond Parfait, Bayberry, Maple Syrup, Lemon Custard, Lavender Sachet, Honeycomb, Wicker White, Paisley Blue

BRUSHES:
No. 4 and No. 6 flat or shader, No. 1 liner, No. 3 round

OTHER MATERIALS:
Wooden bread board

Instructions

Before beginning, read general instructions for Folk Art, on page 12.

1 *Preparation*
Basecoat piece with Green Meadow, allow to dry. Sand lightly with sandpaper. Apply a further coat of paint. Several coats may be needed to cover the piece. Edges of board are painted in Maple Syrup.

2 Transfer pattern onto board using the stylus and white transfer paper.

Painting

3 *Leaves*
Using No. 6 flat brush base in with Bayberry, shade in Green Meadow and highlight in Lemon Custard plus a little Lavender Sachet. Using No. 1 liner, outline leaves in Green Meadow.

4 *Stems*
Using No. 1 liner, mix equal parts of Maple Syrup and Lavender Sachet, paint stems. Outline in Maple Syrup.

5 *Gumnuts*
Using No. 3 round brush, base in with Honeycomb and a little Wicker White. Using No. 4 flat brush, shade in Maple Syrup, highlight in Wicker White. Using No. 1 liner, outline in Maple Syrup.

6 *Babies*
Using No. 3 round brush base in with Almond Parfait, allow to dry. Apply a second coat of Almond Parfait with a little Lemon Custard. Using No. 4 flat brush, shade in Honeycomb and highlight in Wicker White. Using No. 1 liner brush, outline in Maple Syrup.

EYES: Using No. 1 liner brush use Paisley Blue, Wicker White and outline in Maple Syrup.

HATS: Using No. 3 round brush, base in with Bayberry. Using No. 4 flat brush, shade in Green Meadow, highlight with Wicker White. Using No. 1 liner brush, outline in Green Meadow.

FRILL: With No. 3 round brush, base in with Lemon Custard. Using No. 4 flat brush, highlight with Wicker White. With No. 1 liner brush, outline in Maple Syrup.

WINGS: No. 3 round brush with Wicker White.

7 *Spider*
Using No. 3 round brush, base in with Licorice, highlight with Wicker White, using No. 1 liner brush.

8 *Lady bug*
Using No. 3 round brush, base in with Lemon Custard. Finish linework with No. 1 liner brush and Maple Syrup.

Finishing

9 When dry, apply 2 coats of FolkArt Satin Finish Waterbase Varnish.

Section 1

Section 2

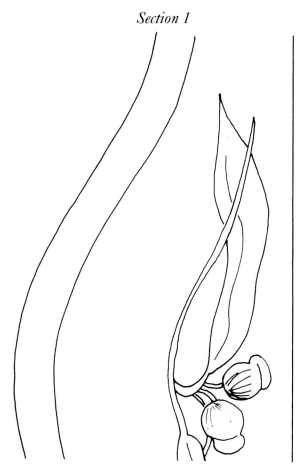

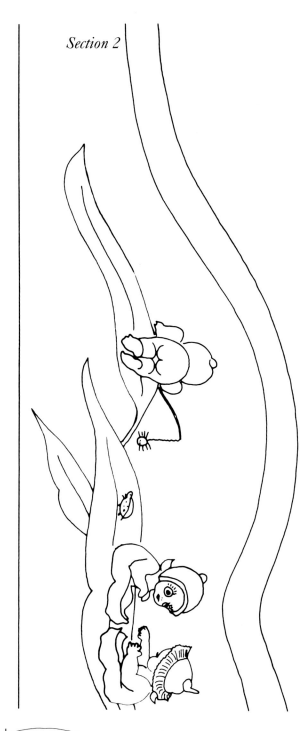

Sections 1 and 2 are the actual size. Trace them and join together, referring to the layout plan below.

Layout plan

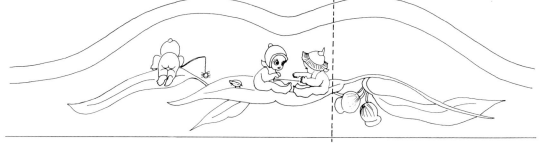

Snugglepot & Cuddlepie Candlesticks

Découpage Gumnut Babies scramble amidst the camouflage of a sponged background on these pretty cottage candlesticks.

Materials

As listed under Découpage Basic Materials, on page 8.

BASE COLOUR:
FolkArt Acrylic Colour: Bayberry

PAINT:
FolkArt Acrylic Colours: Green Meadow, Licorice

BRUSHES:
No. 8 flat

OTHER MATERIALS:
Two wooden candlesticks, sponge brush, small sea sponge, palette, Simson paper featuring Gumnut Babies (no. SC 503G)

Instructions

Before beginning, read general instructions for Découpage, on page 8.

1 *Preparation and Sponging*
Sand the candlesticks, paying particular attention to the inside rim where the candles will be placed.

2 Use the sponge brush to apply 2 coats of Bayberry, allowing to dry and sanding lightly between coats.

3 The next step involves the sponging of the candlesticks. If you have never attempted this background, it may be helpful to practise on paper before you apply this new skill to the candlesticks.

Begin by squeezing a small amount of Green Meadow onto the palette, then dip a pre-moistened sea sponge into the paint. Bounce the sponge up and down on a piece of paper towel to remove excess paint, then touch the sponge to the curved surface of the candlesticks so that an impression is left behind. Lift the sponge and rotate your hand before placing it down onto the candlesticks in a different position. Be sure not to rotate the sponge while it is in contact with the wooden surface, or twist marks will appear instead of a nice crisp print.

Repeat this process until the whole candlestick is sponged with Green Meadow. It should still be possible to see the Bayberry basecoat through the sponging.

Repeat this procedure with the Licorice paint a little more sparingly.

4 Use the No. 8 flat brush to trim the candlesticks with Green Meadow.

5 *Découpage and finishing*
Select the Gumnut Babies from the papers and refer to the general instructions on Découpage on page 8 to complete the project.

*This is a sample of
the Simson paper
used for the
Snugglepot and
Cuddlepie
Candlesticks.*

Country Dining

This delightful folk art motif features Little Ragged Blossom
and her Gumnut companion.

Materials

As listed under Folk Art Basic Materials,
on page 12.

BASE COLOUR:
Stained pine timber with Green Meadow
wash

PAINT:
FolkArt Acrylic Colours: Almond Parfait,
Paisley Blue, Honeycomb, Maple Syrup,
Harvest Gold, Lemon Custard, Green
Meadow, Licorice, Wicker White

BRUSHES:
No. 4 and No. 6 flat or shader
No. 1 liner, No. 3 round

OTHER MATERIALS:
Finished pine dining chairs, sponge
(natural or synthetic)

Instructions

Before beginning, read general instructions
for Folk Art, on page 12.

1 Preparation
Apply 1 coat of FolkArt Satin Finish
Waterbase Varnish to the back of the chair,
in the area to be painted. When dry, using
a sponge, apply Green Meadow mixed
with a little water over the pattern area.

2 Allow to dry, then transfer pattern using
the stylus and transfer paper.

Painting
3 Leaves
Using No. 6 flat brush, base in with Green
Meadow, shade in Maple Syrup and
highlight in Wicker White. Using No. 1
liner brush, outline in Green Meadow and
paint stems in Maple Syrup.

4 Gumnuts
Using No. 3 round brush, base in with
Harvest Gold. With No. 4 flat brush, shade
in Maple Syrup and highlight in Wicker
White with No. 1 liner brush. Outline in
Maple Syrup.

5 Tables and stools
Using No. 3 round brush, base in with a
mix of 1 part Maple Syrup and 1 part
Almond Parfait. Using No. 4 flat brush,
shade in Maple Syrup and highlight with
Harvest Gold.

6 Babies
Using No. 3 round brush, base in with
Almond Parfait, allow to dry. Apply a
second coat of a mix of 1 part Almond
Parfait and 1 part Lemon Custard. Using
No. 4 flat brush, shade in Honeycomb and
highlight with Wicker White. Using No. 1
liner brush, outline in Maple Syrup.
EYES: Paisley Blue, Wicker White and
outline in Maple Syrup.
LASHES: Maple Syrup.
DRESS: Using No. 3 round brush, basecoat
in Lemon Custard, shade in Maple Syrup
and highlight in Wicker White.
WINGS: No. 3 round brush with Wicker
White.

7 Finishing
When dry, apply 2 coats of FolkArt Satin
Finish Waterbase Varnish.

Sections 1 and 2 are
the actual size. Trace
them and join
together, referring
to the layout
plan above.

Layout plan

Section 1

Section 2

Blossom Baby Key Holder

*Blossom Baby and her little feathered friend
Blue-cap take turns to watch over your keys.*

Materials

As listed under Folk Art Basic Materials,
on page 12.

BASE COLOUR:
FolkArt Acrylic Colour: Green Meadow
PAINT:
FolkArt Acrylic Colours: Bayberry, Ripe
Avocado, Wintergreen, Almond Parfait,
Molasses, Harvest Gold, Licorice, Blue
Ribbon, Coastal Blue, Wicker White
BRUSHES:
No. 3 round, No. 8 flat, No. 00 liner
OTHER MATERIALS:
Wooden key holder

Instructions

Before beginning, read general instructions
for Folk Art, on page 12.

1 Preparation
Use the sponge brush to apply 2 to 3 even
basecoats of Green Meadow to key holder,
sanding lightly between coats.

2 Apply a trim of Bayberry around the
edges of the key holder.

3 Transfer pattern onto key holder using
stylus and white transfer paper.

Painting
4 Leaves
Use either No. 8 flat or No. 3 round brush
to apply 2 coats of Bayberry. Allow to dry
between coats. Side-load No. 8 flat brush,
then float Ripe Avocado on left side of
leaves. Wintergreen is floated on the right
side of the leaves.

5 Blossom Baby
Base in with Almond Parfait. When
painting a pale colour over the top of a
dark colour, it may be necessary to apply
3 coats for complete opaque coverage.
Side-load No. 8 flat brush with Molasses
and shade under the chin, arms, and right
leg with a float of Molasses.
HAIR AND SKIRT: A wash of Harvest Gold
forms the base. Then add fine lines of
Harvest Gold pulled with the No. 00 liner
brush. The next layer of lines is a mix of
Harvest Gold and Wicker White and lastly
plain Wicker White. Add tiny dots of
Wicker White in and around the skirt.
HAT: Base in with Bayberry, applying
2 coats. Shade with float of Wintergreen
side-loaded on No. 8 flat brush.
BABY'S FEATURES: Outline with thinned
Licorice or Molasses, using the No. 00
liner brush.

6 Bird
Refer to the coloured photographs for
colour placements.
    Load No. 3 round brush in Licorice to
paint in the darkest sections. Base in blue
areas with Blue Ribbon, applying two
coats if necessary.

When dry, highlight the top of head and upper sections of blue with a float of Coastal Blue, using No. 8 Flat brush.

EYE: Wicker White with a dot of Licorice.

WING: A brush mix of Harvest Gold and Molasses, blended to a dark gold brown painted with No. 3 round brush, then outlined with Molasses using No. 00 liner brush.

LEG: The top of the leg is Harvest Gold with a touch of Molasses to begin with, but adding more Molasses as you move closer to the bird's chest.

Paint the area above the wing Harvest Gold with a touch of Wicker White and a touch of Molasses, using No. 3 round brush. It may help to work some Extender into the brush when blending colours in this way.

CHEST: Licorice with a touch of Molasses using No. 3 round brush. Add a float of Licorice down left side to shade using No. 8 flat brush.

7 *Stems*

Stems are pulled with No. 00 liner brush and paint thinned with water and Extender. Load the brush in Molasses, then add a line of Bayberry above this to make the stems stand out.

8 *Finishing*

When dry, apply 2 coats of FolkArt Satin Finish Waterbase Varnish.

This diagram is the correct size. Trace and transfer to the key holder.

COLOUR CHART

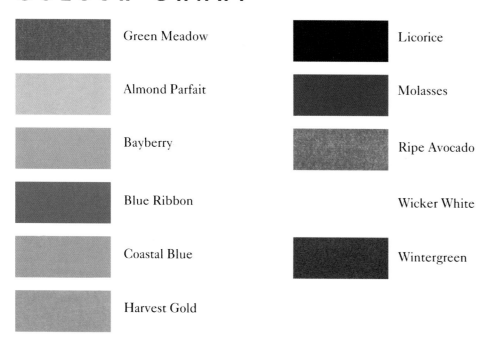

Green Meadow

Almond Parfait

Bayberry

Blue Ribbon

Coastal Blue

Harvest Gold

Licorice

Molasses

Ripe Avocado

Wicker White

Wintergreen

Bush Folk Platter

Fluffy Wattle Babies and Gumnut Babies give this découpaged platter its distinctively Australian colours.

Materials

As listed under Découpage Basic Materials, on page 8.

BASE COLOUR:
FolkArt Acrylic Colour: Green Meadow

OTHER MATERIALS:
Large platter, Simson paper featuring Gumnut Babies (no. SC503G) and Wattle Babies (SC504), sponge brush

Instructions

Before beginning, read general instructions for Découpage, on page 8.

1 *Preparation*
Sand any rough edges of the platter and spray lightly with FolkArt All Purpose Spray to seal.

2 Using the sponge brush, apply 2 or 3 even coats of FolkArt Green Meadow. Allow to dry and sand lightly between coats.

3 *Découpage*
Set out the leaves and Gumnut Babies by referring to the photograph, or arrange the pictures to your own taste.

4 Apply Mod Podge and glue cutouts in place. In this project, the papers do not overlap, so it is possible to work quite quickly once the design has been selected.

5 *Varnishing and Finishing*
Once you are satisfied that the gluing process is complete, begin the build-up of layers of Mod Podge, brushing from the outside edge, across the centre of the platter to the opposite edge. Each time a layer of Mod Podge is added, turn the platter so that you begin in a different position. This will allow for an even build-up of glue and cover all angles of the paper as you rotate around the plate.

6 When sanding with the wet and dry paper, press very lightly, allowing a good cushion of water between the platter and the sandpaper so that the sandpaper glides across the platter. Pay particular attention to the curved ridge of the platter as extra pressure in this spot could lead to a tear in the découpage paper.

7 Continue with the build-up of Mod Podge, then varnish as outlined in the general instructions (pages 8 to 9). Finish the piece by waxing and buffing to a deep soft glow.

These are samples of the Simson papers used for the Bush Folk Platter.

Bush Babies Place Mat

A charming and practical place mat makes an ideal and inexpensive introduction to the art of stencilling.

Materials

As listed under Stencilling Basic Materials, on page 10.

BASE COLOUR:
French Wash Wall Wash: Celadon Green

PAINT:
Artist Paint Crayons: Wild Ivy Green, Wildflower Honey, Ol' Pioneer Red, Victorian Rose, Promenade Rose (optional)

OTHER MATERIALS:
Pre-primed canvas (from artists' supplies) set square, chalk pencil, kneadable rubber, small sea sponge, small bowl, small stencil brushes, FolkArt Waterbase Varnish Satin Finish, Founders Adhesive Glue, rolling pin, masking tape

Instructions

Before beginning, read general instructions for Stencilling, on page 10.

1 *Preparation*

Cut a piece of pre-primed canvas, 420 cm by 300 cm. Use a chalk pencil to mark a border 4 cm around the whole rectangle, then mark another rectangle 6 cm inside that. These areas will form the border and the centre area for sponging, leaving a band of white.

2

To protect this area from paint while sponging, it will be necessary to mask off both sides of the plain band with masking tape. Be sure that the corners meet accurately and press down firmly along the edges with your fingernail.

3 *Sponging*

Shake the bottle of French Wash well to mix the paint, then pour a small quantity into a bowl. Dip a moist sea sponge into the bowl and pick up some paint. It may be necessary to squeeze out excess to prevent drips. Pounce up and down on a piece of paper to remove excess, then sponge the outside border and the inner section making sure that no paint has come over the edges into the white area. If there are any blots, remove the paint while it is still wet. Remember to rotate your hand after each pounce of the sponge, to avoid a repetitive pattern, but be sure to lift your hand before turning it so that twist marks don't appear. Remove the masking tape. Allow to dry and remove any outlines with kneadable rubber.

4 *Preparing and cutting the stencil*

Prepare stencils, following general instructions, on page 10.

There will be four stencils required: 1) green leaves and hat; 2) stems; 3) yellow leaves and hair; 4) babies.

Remember to trace grid placement lines.

5 *Stencilling*

Position the stencil on the place mat, checking that it is lined up accurately in

the white border area.

LEAVES: Begin with the Wild Ivy Green leaves and hat, working in small circles as you brush on the paint. Next paint the Wildflower Honey leaves and hair. Ol' Pioneer Red is blended in on some of the leaves. By placing the stems on top of the last two stencils the veins appear to be more prominent.

BABIES: Paint with Victorian Rose, but try a blush of Promenade Rose brushed over their bottoms, if desired.

6 *Finishing*

Allow the paint to dry for a day or two before finishing off with 2 or 3 coats of FolkArt Satin Waterbase Varnish.

7 The hem of 2 cm can be turned under and glued down using Founders Adhesive Glue. Mitre the corners for a neat look and use a rolling pin to ensure crisp edges.

This diagram shows the position of the illustration on the mat.

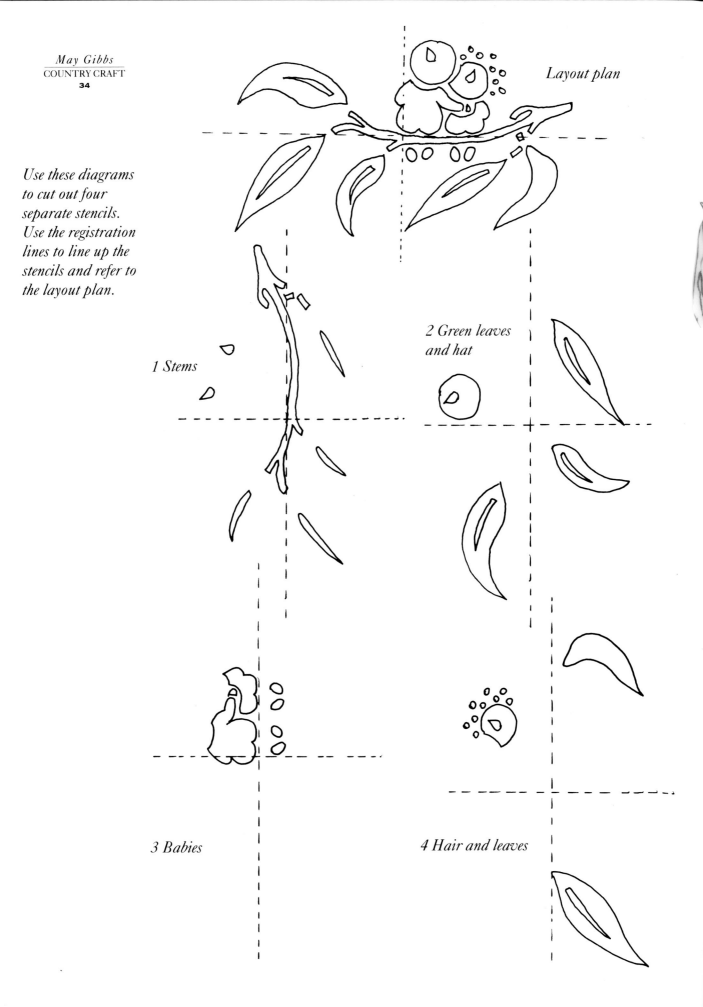

Layout plan

Use these diagrams
to cut out four
separate stencils.
Use the registration
lines to line up the
stencils and refer to
the layout plan.

1 Stems

*2 Green leaves
and hat*

3 Babies

4 Hair and leaves

Bushland Serviette Rings

The simplest leaf and gum blossom make this dainty painted serviette ring an ideal project for beginners. It coordinates beautifully with the Bush Babies Place Mat.

This motif is actual size. Trace and transfer to the serviette ring.

Materials

As listed under Folk Art Basic Materials on page 12.

BASE COLOUR:
FolkArt Acrylic Colour: Green Meadow

PAINT:
FolkArt Acrylic Colours: Green Meadow, Bayberry, Wintergreen, Molasses, Sunny Yellow, Buttercup, Wicker White
FolkArt extender

BRUSHES:
No. 3 round, No. 8 flat, 00 liner, sponge brush

OTHER MATERIALS:
Wooden serviette ring

Instructions

Before beginning, read general instructions for Folk Art, on page 12.

1 Preparation
Basecoat with 2 coats of Green Meadow, using the sponge brush and allowing to dry between coats. Trim the edges with Bayberry.

2
Transfer motif to the serviette ring, using stylus and white transfer paper.

Painting

3 Leaf
Base with two coats of Bayberry, using No. 3 round brush. Allow to dry. Float Wintergreen on the lower edge of the leaf, then float Molasses on the top edge, using No. 8 flat brush.

Load No. 00 liner brush in Molasses and, beginning at the stem end, pull a fine line to mark the centre vein. Paint a comma-like stroke for the gumnut.

4 Blossoms
Paint with No. 00 liner brush, beginning with Buttercup. Pull fine lines from the gumnut. Next, paint in Sunny Yellow lines and lastly Wicker White adding Wicker White dots just beyond the end of the lines.

5 Finishing
Allow to dry, then brush on two coats of FolkArt Satin Finish Waterbase Varnish.

Bush Folk at Home

Create this delightful child's room with our wall frieze and Height Chart, Coathangers and Wall Plaque. We have also used May Gibbs fabric to make a pillow case and May Gibbs paper to découpage a trolley and some blocks to brighten up the room. The practical and decorative mat has been sponged, stencilled and painted with folk art.

Welcome to May's Room

What small child could resist the shy, peeping glances of the Gumnut Babies on this pretty personalised folk art wall plaque?

Materials

As listed under Folk Art Basic Materials, on page 12.

BASECOLOUR:
FolkArt Acrylic Colour: Dove Grey

PAINT:
FolkArt Acrylic Colours: Tartan Green, Ripe Avocado, Bayberry, Wintergreen, Brownie, Molasses, Taffy, Almond Parfait, Blue Grey Dust, Teal Blue, Porcelain Blue, Icy White, Celadon Green

BRUSHES:
No. 00 liner, No. 3 round, No. 8 flat

OTHER MATERIALS:
Wooden wall plaque, FolkArt All Purpose Spray

Instructions

Before beginning, read general instructions for Folk Art, on page 12.

1 *Preparation*
Apply 2 smooth coats of Dove Grey. Sand between coats, paying particular attention to the outside rim.

2 Brush the surface with Extender then scumble, that is, roughly and unevenly brush on Porcelain Blue, Teal Blue, Icy White, and Celadon Green, so that the colours blend together but do not merge. Allow to dry then spray with All Purpose Spray.

3 Float Brownie around the rim of plaque.

4 Transfer pattern to plaque, using stylus and white transfer paper.

Painting
5 *Leaves*
Using No. 8 flat brush and beginning with the leaf in background, base in with Blue Grey Dust.

Leaf 2: leave the colour in the brush and pick up Bayberry.

Leaf 3: keeping the previous colours in the brush, pick up Tartan Green, adding more Tartan Green for leaves 4 and 5 until Leaf 6 is all Tartan Green.

Leaf 7: the foreground leaf is Bayberry. Leaf 1 is shaded with a float of Brownie; Leaf 2 has a shade of Brownie and a highlight of Blue Grey Dust; Leaf 3 is shaded with Tartan Green and has a tint of Ripe Avocado. Leaves 4, 5 and 6 are shaded with Wintergreen. Leaf 7, the Bayberry leaf, is shaded with Brownie.

6 Most of the veins on the leaves are Brownie, pulled with No. 00 liner brush, while the leaf tips in the background are Taffy.

7 The border, leaves and the writing are painted using No. 00 liner brush, loaded in thinned Brownie.

8 *Babies*
Using No. 3 round brush, base in with Almond Parfait, then shade in thinned Molasses and outline in thinned Molasses. Brush highlights of Taffy over their shoulders. Their tiny wings are Taffy.

Hats: Using No. 3 round brush, base in Bayberry, adding Wintergreen shading and touches of Molasses to deepen the shading. Tints of Ripe Avocado accent the centres of the caps.

9 *Finishing*
Apply 2 or 3 coats of FolkArt Satin Finish Waterbase Varnish and attach hooks or a hanger.

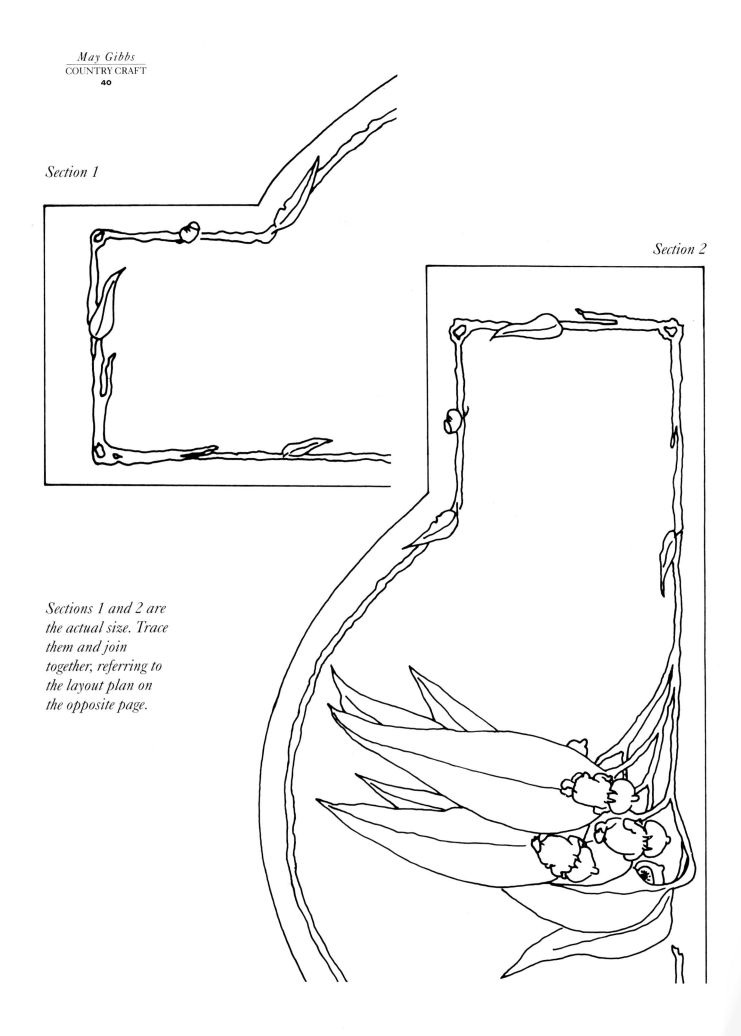

Section 1

Section 2

*Sections 1 and 2 are
the actual size. Trace
them and join
together, referring to
the layout plan on
the opposite page.*

Layout plan

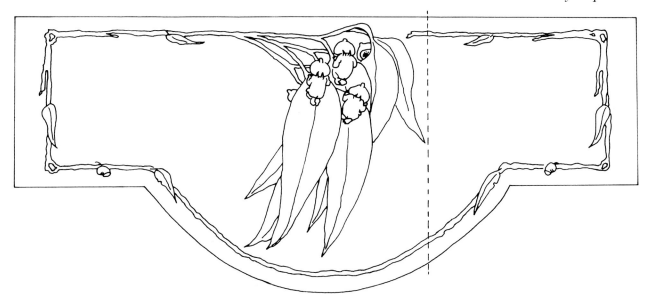

C O L O U R   C H A R T

Dove Grey

Almond Parfait

Bayberry

Blue Gray Dust

Brownie

Celadon Green

Icy White

Molasses

Porcelain Blue

Ripe Avocado

Taffy

Tartan Green

Teal Blue

Wintergreen

Scrumbled Background

Little Obelia's Coathangers

Tots will adore these pint-sized hangers, finished in your choice of stencilling, folk art or découpage.

1. Folk Art Coathanger

Materials

As listed under Folk Art Basic Materials, on page 12.

BASE COLOUR:
FolkArt Acrylic Colour: Buttercream

PAINT:
FolkArt Acrylic Colours: Buttercup, Almond Parfait, Molasses, Bayberry, Tartan Green, Sunny Yellow, Gingersnap, Pimento

BRUSHES:
No. 3 round, No. 00 liner, No. 4 flat

OTHER MATERIALS:
Wooden coathanger, plastic tubing, ribbon

Instructions

Before beginning, read general instructions for Folk Art, on page 12.

1 *Preparation*
Basecoat the coathanger with 2 coats of Buttercream, with a float of Buttercup around the outside edge.

Painting
2 *Babies*
SKIN: Use No. 3 round brush to base in with Almond Parfait, shade with Molasses using No. 4 flat brush, then outline in Molasses with No. 00 liner brush.
HATS: Use Bayberry based with No. 3 round brush, shaded with Tartan Green using No. 4 flat brush; outline in Tartan Green.

3 *Caterpillar*
Use the No. 4 flat brush to base and shade and highlight the Caterpillar. Base in with Bayberry and shade in the folds of the legs with Tartan Green. Highlight along the top of the body with Sunny Yellow. Deepen the shading behind the baby's leg with Molasses. With No. 00 liner brush, outline in a brush mix of Tartan Green and Molasses.

Reins and whip are Molasses linework.

4 *Beetles*
SHELL: Paint back with No. 4 flat brush in Gingersnap, then use same brush to shade on top with Pimento and underneath with Molasses. The line near the base is Molasses and legs are Molasses, painted with No. 00 liner brush.

The front of the shell is a mix of Pimento and Sunny Yellow, outlined in Sunny Yellow. You may use No. 00 liner brush in these small areas.
HEAD: Sunny Yellow, shaded underneath with Molasses.
LEGS AND FEELERS: Use Molasses on the No. 00 Liner brush.

5 *Finishing*
When dry, apply 2 coats of FolkArt Satin Finish Waterbase Varnish. Slip white plastic tubing over metal hook, then tie a coordinating ribbon around hook to add a dainty touch.

2. Stencilled Coathanger

Materials

As listed under Stencilling Basic Materials, on page 10.

BASE COLOUR:
FolkArt Acrylic Colour: Buttercream

PAINT:
Artist Paint crayons: Ship's Fleet Navy, Wildflower Honey, Truffles Brown, Ol' Pioneer Red

OTHER MATERIALS:
Wooden coathanger, small stencil brushes sea sponge, sponge brush

Instructions

Before beginning, read general instructions for Stencilling, on page 10.

1 *Preparation*
Basecoat the coathanger in Buttercream, then sponge on Buttercup.

2 Prepare stencils following general instructions, on page 10.
There are a number of small cuts for each section of the butterflies' wings. Look closely at the photograph to check that you have not missed any sections or colours.

3 *Stencilling*
Stencil the two brown bodies and remember to turn the stencil over to stencil the mirror image of the first butterfly.

4 The Wildflower Honey body and wings are next.

5 Stencil wings in Ol' Pioneer Red next, again remembering to turn the stencil over for the righthand butterfly.

6 Finally, stencil wings on both the right and left side in Ship's Fleet Navy.

7 *Finishing*
Allow several days for the oil paint to dry before varnishing with 2 coats of FolkArt Satin Finish Waterbase Varnish. Slip white plastic tubing over metal hook, then tie a coordinating ribbon around hook to add a dainty touch.

3. Découpage Coathanger

Materials

As listed under Découpage Basic Materials, on page 8.

BASE COLOUR:
FolkArt Acrylic Colour: Buttercream

OTHER MATERIALS:
Wooden coathanger, Simson papers featuring Gumnut Babies (no.SC 503 G), sponge brush.

Instructions

Before beginning, read general instructions for Découpage, on page 8.

1 *Preparation*
Basecoat in Buttercream and apply trim of Buttercup to the outside edge of the coathanger.

2 *Découpage*
Select the appropriate motifs and cut them, following general instructions, on page 8.

3 Apply the Mod Podge to the hanger and add the motifs in the positions you prefer. Turn back to the general instructions on page 8 and complete in the usual manner.

4 *Finishing*
Apply varnish then wax to a smooth finish. Slip white plastic tubing over metal hook, then tie a coordinating ribbon around hook to add a dainty touch.

This a reduced version of the Stencilled Coathanger. Refer to the pull-out pattern sheet for the actual diagrams.

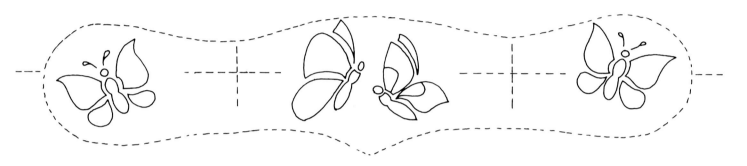

COLOUR CHART

	FolkArt Colours		Basecoat Colour
	Almond Parfait	Sunny Yellow	Buttercream
	Bayberry	Tartan Green	
	Buttercup	**Stencilling Colours** Ship's Fleet Navy	
	Gingersnap	Wildflower Honey	
	Molasses (Beetles)	Truffles Brown	
	Pimento	Ol' Pioneer Red	

This is a sample of the Simson paper used for the Découpage Coathanger.

This diagram shows the position of the picture on the Découpage Coathanger.

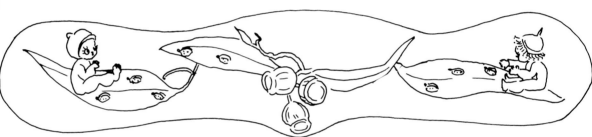

These diagrams are actual size. Trace them and transfer to the coathanger, referring to the reduced layout below.

Bush Folk Wall Frieze

Bring a little May Gibbs magic to a child's room with a stencilled wall frieze, featuring Possum and the Gumnut Babies. Repeat the motif on coordinating bedroom accessories to complete the theme.

Materials

As listed under Stencilling Basic Materials, on page 10.

BASE COLOUR:
French Wash Wall Wash: Celadon Green and Sky Blue

PAINT:
Artist Paint Crayons: Wild Ivy Green, Ship's Fleet Navy, Ol' Pioneer Red, Cameo Peach, Promenade Rose, Truffles Brown, Vintage Burgundy, Turtle Dove Grey, Andiron Black

OTHER MATERIALS:
Pen and ink eraser, set square/spirit level, metal tape-measure, chalk pencil, stencil brushes (one for each colour), small bowl, sea sponge, Masking tape

Instructions

Before beginning, read the general instructions for Stencilling, on page 10. Note: When stencilling the wall frieze, keep in mind the positioning for the Bush Folk Height Chart. This chart joins onto the wall frieze by simply leaving out the Possum, and Baby and Blossom overlays. The height chart possum's tail links over the branch on which the Baby sits. Look at the photograph for clarification.

1 *Preparing the stencil*
Prepare stencils, following general instructions, on page 10, and using the actual diagrams on the pull-out pattern sheet.

This project requires four different overlays: 1) Stems; 2) Leaves and Hat; 3) Possum; 4) Gumnut Baby and Blossoms.

2 *Preparing the wall*
Any painted surface can be stencilled as long as it does not have a high gloss finish. This room has been sponged up to the height of the stencil using French Wash.

3 Measure up from the floor 120 cm and draw a line with the chalk pencil, checking that the line is level with a spirit level. It is possible to mask above this line with low tack masking tape, to protect this area from over-sponging. This line also provides the maximum height of the Bush Folk Height Chart in the following project.

4 Mix equal quantities of Sky Blue and Celadon Green in a small bowl. Use a sea sponge to sponge on a soft look following the instructions for sponging described in past projects. Allow the sponging time to dry before beginning the stencilling.

5 *Stencilling*
Before stencilling directly on the wall, it is a good idea to prepare a paper proof. This is used as a 'test sample' of the design and your stencilling technique before applying it to the wall. It will help you to understand the repeats and overlays of the

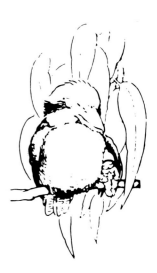

stencil. It also enables you to check the colours in the room and can be used as an aid to measurement.

6 Most stencil designs begin in a room's most dominant corner and end in a corner on the door wall. The most dominant corner is usually the corner opposite the entrance doorway.

It is often a good idea to lay protective sheeting on the floor to prevent any marks caused by dropping paint crayons. Remember that these are oil paints in stick form and it would be very difficult to remove marks from carpets. After checking that the horizontal line drawn for the sponging is level, and after testing the wall length with the stencilled proof to determine where you may need to 'stretch and squeeze' (see page 10) you will be ready to begin stencilling.

7 *Stems*
Begin with stems using Truffles Brown. Remember to work in tight circles, to brush on the paint evenly.

8 *Leaves and Hat*
Work these next in Wild Ivy Green. Shadings of Ship's Fleet Navy have been brushed onto the top left side of the leaves while a highlight of Ol' Pioneer Red has added interest towards the tips of the leaves.

9 *Possum*
Base in Turtle Dove Grey with a shading of Andiron Black down the left side. On the Possum's right side and tail, add a warm touch with Truffles Brown. If you wish, a tiny touch of Promenade Rose can give the tip of his nose a pink glow.

10 On the last sheet you will need to work carefully, as two colours are to be used on the one sheet. First, brush in the Baby with Cameo Peach. Next, work the blossoms in Vintage Burgundy, being careful not to overbrush the Baby. If in doubt, cover the Baby with a piece of masking tape to protect it from the deeper pink. The Babies do look very nice if a slight blush of the deeper pink wisps over their bottoms.

11 Check your work before progressing too far and if there are any overstrokes, erase them with the ink rubber.

12 *Finishing*
Since the Paint Crayons are oil-based, the stencilling does not need to be sealed. It does need to be left to dry for several days, however, to harden and cure. Once this has happened, grubby finger marks can be wiped away with a damp cloth without damaging the stencilling.

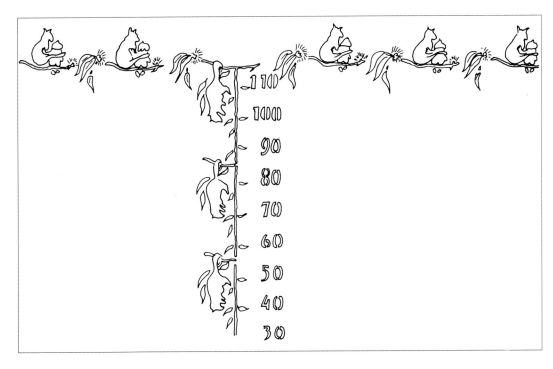

120
1·10
1·00
·90
·80
·70
·60
·50
·40
·30
·20
·10
0

Bush Folk Height Chart

This height chart was designed to coordinate with Bush Folk Wall Frieze, using the same colours and techniques. Young children love to record how much they have grown and will find it great fun to measure themselves against Mr Possum and the Gumnut Babies.

Materials

As listed under Stencilling Basic Materials, on page 10.

BASE COLOUR:
French Wash Wall Wash: Celadon Green and Sky Blue (see Bush Folk Wall Frieze)

PAINT:
Artist Paint Crayons: Wildflower Honey, Wild Ivy Green, Ship's Fleet Navy, Ol' Pioneer Red, Cameo Peach, Promenade Rose, Truffles Brown, Vintage Burgundy, Turtle Dove Grey, Andiron Black

OTHER MATERIALS:
Simply Stencils Pre-cut, 2" Numbers, pen and ink eraser, ruler and set square, metal tape-measure, chalk pencil, stencil brushes (one for each colour)

Instructions

Before beginning, read the general instructions, on page 10.

1 *Preparing the stencil*
Refer to the actual diagrams on the pull-out pattern sheet. When stencilling the Bush Folk Wall Frieze, keep in mind the positioning for the height chart. This chart joins onto the wall frieze by simply leaving out the Possum, and Baby and Blossom overlays. The height chart possum's tail links over the branch on which the Baby sits. Look at the photograph for clarification. Prepare the stencils, following general instructions, on page 10. Cut four stencils, as for wall frieze.

2 *Measuring the wall*
Use the set square to draw a vertical line down the wall at 90 degrees to the original horizontal line you drew at 120 cm from the floor.

On the stencil, marker leaves are placed every 10 cm down the wall. Measure these 10 cm intervals and holding the set square at right angles to the vertical line, draw lines with the chalk pencil to indicate the positioning of the numerals.

3 *Stencilling*
Make a paper proof of this stencil and hold it against the wall to check spacing.

4 Follow the colour steps for the Stencilled Wall Frieze, adding Wildflower Honey for the Baby's hair.
   Stencil the numerals in Ship's Fleet Navy. Refer to the photograph for placement.
   (Note if you wish to make your own numbers, use the templates below).

5 Check your work before progressing too far and if there are any overstrokes, erase them with the ink rubber.

6 *Finishing*
Since the Paint Crayons are oil-based, the stencilling does not need to be sealed. It does need to be left to dry for several days, however, to harden and cure. Once this has happened, grubby finger marks can be wiped away with a damp cloth without damaging the stencilling.

These numbers are actual size. Trace and cut out stencils.

From a
Country Garden

Country Cushion

Blue delphinium looks spectacular
stencilled on a rustic calico cushion.

Materials

As listed under Stencilling Basic Materials, on page 10.

BASE COLOUR:
French Wash Wall Wash: Sky Blue and Celadon Green

PAINT:
FolkArt Acrylic Colours: Blue Ribbon, Bluegrass

OTHER MATERIALS:
40 cm x 120 cm wide calico, 140 cm purchased or self-made contrast piping, FolkArt Textile Medium, plastic sheet, medium stencil brushes, small bowl, small sea sponge, 25 cm zip, 30 cm cushion insert, chalk pencil

Instructions

Before beginning, read general instructions for Stencilling, on page 10.

1 *Preparation*

Wash the calico in the washing machine to remove fabric sizing. Iron the fabric to smooth it, then cut one 34 cm square for cushion front and two 34 cm x 19 cm rectangles for cushion backs.

2 Stretch front out on a firm surface with a protective sheet of plastic underneath. Pour an equal quantity of Sky Blue and Celadon Green Wall Wash into a small bowl and mix thoroughly. Load the moistened sponge in the Wall Wash, squeeze to remove excess paint, then sponge the fabric with this blue-green mix.

3 When the calico is dry, use a chalk pencil to mark the centre lines, then draw a border 2 cm around outside edge of the square. This will provide seam allowance when sewing the cushion.

Also draw lines to mark the centres on each side, to help with lining up the stencil.

4 *Preparing the stencil*

Prepare stencils, following general instructions on page 10. You will notice that the stencil is drawn as a mirror image, one part on the left, one on the right. Don't forget to mark the centre lines, and side lines so that you will be able to line up the stencil sheet with the lines on the cushion. Make sure that you have left a 2 cm border around the edge of the stencil to prevent overbrushing on the project. It will be necessary to cut 2 stencils for this project, 1 for the flowers and 1 for the foliage.

5 *Stencilling*

Check that the Wall Wash decoration is dry and that centre marks have been marked lightly in chalk pencil.

6 Begin stencilling the foliage, preparing the paint by mixing 2 parts Bluegrass with 1 part Textile Medium.

7 Allow the paint to dry before beginning the second colour. Mix Blue Ribbon with the Textile Medium in the above proportion and after checking that the registration lines are properly aligned, brush on the colour for the flowers.

8 Work left side of the cushion first, allow it to dry, then proceed to the right side. It would help ensure a clean job if the stencils were washed between sides. Dry both the overlay sheets and the brushes before re-using.

9 *Finishing*

When the project has dried, permanently set the paint by ironing the back with a heat setting appropriate to the textile you have used.

10 *Making up the cushion*

With right sides facing, stitch piping around cushion front, nicking piping seam allowance at the corners for ease and stitching along marked 2 cm seam line. To overlap piping ends and prevent bulk, draw out that portion of the cord that will overlap and cut it off. Straighten out the piping ends and finish stitching, being sure to take the piping ends off at an angle into the seam allowance to conceal them. Place backing pieces together, right sides facing and raw edges even, and stitch across one 34 cm edge, taking a 2 cm allowance and leaving a 25 cm gap in the centre for zip insertion. Open out backs, press seam open and insert zip. Leave zip open.

Place cushion back and front together, right sides facing, and stitch around outside, following stitching line for piping. Turn cover right side out through zip and insert cushion.

These diagrams show the combined stencil pattern. Refer to the pull-out pattern sheet for the diagrams to make stencils from.

This layout plan shows the position of the design on the cushion.

Blossoms and Lace

This quick and easy découpage bookmark is an easy project for a beginner, and is a wonderful way to use up leftovers from other projects.

Materials

As listed under Découpage Basic Materials, on page 8, except bookmark is not waxed to finish.

BASE COLOUR:
FolkArt Acrylic BaseCoat: Wicker White

PAINT:
French Wash Wall Wash: Sky Blue

OTHER MATERIALS:
Strong cardboard or two pieces of cereal box cut to the same size, 50 cm cotton lace, beaded edging, 50 cm fine pale blue ribbon, Simson paper featuring Blue Bell Babies (no. SC505), Founder's Adhesive Glue, hole punch

Instructions

Before beginning, read general instructions for Découpage, on page 8.

1 *Preparation of bookmark*
Cut the cardboard to size, then apply several coats of Wicker White BaseCoat. If you have used 2 pieces of cardboard, glue them together with Mod Podge, then paint both sides, one at a time, allowing them to dry between coats.

2 Sponge with Sky Blue Wall Wash, as described for Bush Babies Place Mat (on page 31).

3 Thread the ribbon through lace beading and trim to size. Use Founder's Adhesive to glue the lace to the sides of the bookmark. Cut or punch a hole with a hole punch at the centre top of the bookmark.

4 *Découpage*
Cut out the motifs, and glue to the card, using Mod Podge. Squeeze out excess glue, then coat the card in more layers of Mod Podge, building up to at least 5 coats.

5 Apply 2 to 3 coats of varnish. Allow to dry.

6 Thread the remaining ribbon through the hole in the top and tie it attractively for a personalised bookmark.

Pots of Flowers

Blossom Babies frolic on a sponged background, while a garland of delphiniums decorates a simple pot.

1. The White Pot

This pot requires previous experience or skill.

Materials

As listed under Folk Art Basic Materials, on page 12.

BASE COLOUR:
FolkArt Acrylic BaseCoat: Wicker White
French Wash Wall Wash: Sky Blue

PAINT:
FolkArt Acrylic Colours: Bluegrass, Blue Ribbon, Ultramarine, Midnight, Robin's Egg, Buttercup, Sunny Yellow, Almond Parfait, Taffy, Victorian Rose, Molasses, Licorice, Wicker White

BRUSHES:
No. 8 flat, No. 3 round, No. 00 liner

OTHER MATERIALS:
Terracotta pot, old toothbrush, sea sponge, Mod Podge Matte, small bowl

Instructions

Before beginning, read general instructions for Folk Art, on page 12.

1 *Preparation*
Before pots are decorated, they should be sealed. Sand off any rough spots with sandpaper and wipe with a tack rag to remove any dust. Brush on 2 coats of Mod Podge Matte with a sponge brush. Allow to dry.

2 Apply 2 to 3 coats of Wicker White BaseCoat, allowing to dry between coats.

3 Apply the sponging next. Shake the bottle of French Wash well to distribute the paint, then pour a small quantity into a shallow bowl.
Dip the pre-moistened sponge into the Wall Wash and if necessary, squeeze to remove excess. Sponge with Wall Wash, as described for Bush Babies Place Mat (on page 31). The sponging should appear as a pale blue over the white.

4 Spatter the pot with Bluegrass paint, thinned with Extender. Dip an old raggy toothbrush into the thinned paint, shake the excess out, then flick the bristles so that the paint spatters the surface of the pot. It is a good idea to practise on paper before attempting this finish on a project, especially if you are not familiar with the technique.

5 When dry, transfer pattern to pot, using stylus and grey transfer paper.

Painting

6 *Flowers*

Using the No. 8 flat brush, base in the larger flowers with Blue Ribbon. Use No. 3 round brush for the smaller flowers. Side-load No. 8 flat brush and highlight the edges of some of the petals with Wicker White. Refer to the photograph for placement of the highlights, although they are generally on the upper edges of the flowers.

Wash some tints of Ultramarine over some sections of the flowers with the No. 8 flat brush.

Shade some folds behind petals in Midnight with the No. 8 flat brush. Centre dot is Midnight, while dots on either side of the centre are Buttercup, using the No. 00 liner brush.

7 *Foliage*

Paint in Robin's Egg with No. 00 liner brush, using tiny comma or 's' strokes. When dry overpaint with Bluegrass.

8 *Spider*

Paint in Buttercup, using No. 3 round brush, then highlight with Sunny Yellow. Legs are linework in Licorice.

9 *Babies*

Apply several coats of Almond Parfait with No. 3 round brush. Paint highlights of Taffy on shoulders and upper areas with No. 8 flat brush, side-loaded. Using the same brush, add a washed blush of Victorian Rose to cheeks. Do shading with thinned Molasses.

OUTLINE: Using No. 00 liner brush, paint with Molasses.

EYES: Using No. 00 liner brush, paint with Blue Ribbon.

EYELASHES: Using No. 00 liner brush paint with Licorice.

10 *Finishing*

When the painting is dry, check that all transfer lines have been covered or erased, then apply a coat or two of Mod Podge Matte to seal.

These diagrams are correct size. Trace and transfer to the pot.

Motif for centre of pot

Motif for lip of pot

2. Flower Border Pot

This design requires an intermediate level of experience.

Materials

As listed under Folk Art Basic Materials, on page 12.

BASE COLOUR:
FolkArt Acrylic Colour: Summer Sky

PAINT:
FolkArt Acrylic Colour: Summer Sky, Blue Ribbon, Wicker White, Bluegrass

BRUSHES:
No. 3 round, No. 00 liner, No. 8 flat

OTHER MATERIALS:
Terracotta pot, Mod Podge Matte

Instructions

Before beginning, read general instructions for Folk Art, on page 12.

1 *Preparation*
After preparing the pot as described for White Pot, apply 2 coats of Summer Sky to trim the top edge of the pot. Allow to dry.

2 Transfer pattern to pot, using stylus and white transfer paper. You may need to adjust the spacing a little to make the design fit evenly around your particular pot.

Painting
3 Paint the design, using the No. 3 round brush with comma and 's' strokes. Load the brush in Blue Ribbon, then side-load in Wicker White. As you paint the 's' strokes, keep the white to top side. Don't pick up white with each stroke but let the colour run out as you progress through each section of the flower. This gives a natural shading and highlighting and looks more realistic.

4 The dot in the centre of the flower is Blue Ribbon.

5 *Foliage*
Paint in comma and 's' strokes as well, this time using No. 00 liner brush, loaded in Bluegrass.

6 *Finishing*
After checking that all transfer lines are covered or erased, apply 2 coats of Mod Podge Matte to the rim of the pot.

This diagram is the actual size. Trace and transfer to the pot.

COLOUR CHART

Almond Parfait	Taffy	Sunny Yellow
Bluegrass	Ultramarine	**BASECOLOURS** Wicker White
Blue Ribbon	Victorian Rose	Sky Blue
Buttercup	Molasses	Summer Sky
Licorice	Robin's Egg	
Midnight	Summer Sky	

Little Delphinium Watering Can

Even an old watering can may be transformed with a painted spray of whimsical Delphinium Babies.

Materials

As listed under Folk Art Basic Materials, on page 12.

BASE COLOUR:
FolkArt Acrylic BaseCoat: Tapioca

PAINT:
FolkArt Acrylic Colours: Maple Syrup, Honeycomb, Harvest Gold, Lavender Sachet, Paisley Blue, Holiday Red, Lemon Custard, Almond Parfait, Tapioca, Wicker White

BRUSHES:
No. 6 flat or shader , No. 1 liner or script liner, No. 3 round, No. 4 flat

OTHER MATERIALS:
Metal watering can (old or new), galvanised primer, for new metal, vinegar, water

Instructions

Before beginning, read general instructions for Folk Art, on page 12.

1 Preparation

NEW METAL CAN: Basecoat with a galvanised primer. When dry, basecoat with 2 coats of Satin Finish Waterbase Varnish. Allow to dry, then apply several coats of the base colour, Tapioca.

OLD METAL CAN: Wash with a mixture of equal parts of vinegar and water. Allow to dry, apply 3 coats of Satin Finish Waterbase Varnish. When dry, apply several coats of the base colour, Tapioca.

2 Transfer pattern to watering can, using the stylus and grey transfer paper.

This diagram is the actual size. Trace and transfer to the watering can.

Painting

3 *Leaves*

Using No. 3 round brush, base in all leaves with Honeycomb. Load No. 6 flat brush with Maple Syrup, shade; highlight with Tapioca. Using No. 1 liner brush, outline leaves in Maple Syrup and paint fine stems in Harvest Gold.

4 *Blue flowers*

Using No. 6 flat brush, base in petals with Lavender Sachet, shade with Paisley Blue and highlight with Wicker White and a small amount of Holiday Red. Using No. 1 liner brush, outline petals in Paisley Blue and centres with Lemon Custard and Maple Syrup dots.

5 *Flower baby*

DRESS AND HAT: Paint the same as for the Flowers. Add Lemon Custard and Wicker White trim around face.

BODY: Using No. 3 round brush, base in with Almond Parfait. Using No. 4 flat brush, shade in Honeycomb and highlight in Wicker White. Using No. 1 liner brush, outline in Maple Syrup.

FACE: Using No. 3 round brush, base in with Almond Parfait. Using No. 4 flat brush, shade in Honeycomb and highlight in Wicker White.

EYES: Paisley Blue and Wicker White.

LASHES: Outline in Maple Syrup.

6 *Border trim*

Paint leaves and flowers as previously instructed for the main pattern.

7 *Finishing*

When dry, apply 2 coats of FolkArt Satin Finish Waterbase Varnish.

*This diagram is the
actual size. Trace
and transfer to the
watering can.*

C O L O U R   C H A R T

Almond Parfait

Lavender
Sachet

Harvest Gold

Tapioca

Utramarine

Holiday Red

Lemon Custard

Wicker White

Honeycomb

Maple Syrup

BASECOAT
Tapioca

A Garland of Blossoms

Delicate folk art flowers add a very special touch to the band of a summer hat.

Materials

As listed under Folk Art Basic Materials, on page 12.

PAINT:
FolkArt Acrylic Colours: Green Meadow, Wicker White, Holiday Red, Paisley Blue, Plum Pudding, Lemon Custard

BRUSHES:
No. 1 liner, No. 2 flat

OTHER MATERIALS:
Wide grosgrain ribbon for band

Instructions

Before beginning, read general instructions for Folk Art, on page 12.

1 Preparation
Transfer pattern onto ribbon using stylus and grey transfer paper.

Painting
2 Leaves
Using No. 1 liner brush, load with Green Meadow, and top load with Wicker White, that is, load a small amount of white onto the tip of the brush. Paint all leaves and stems.

3 Flowers
Using No. 4 flat brush, add a small amount of Extender, side-load with a mix of Holiday Red and Paisley Blue (a soft lilac shade); on the opposite side of the brush load with Wicker White.

Blend colours on palette by stroking several times. Paint petals of flowers.

For line work, using No. 1 liner brush, paint in Plum Pudding and use Lemon Custard for centre dot.

4 Apply the ribbon to the band of the hat and secure in place with Founder's Adhesive Glue.

*This diagram is the
actual size. Trace
and transfer to the
hat band.*

Country Garden Apron

*Stencilled flowers bloom on an old-fashioned gardeners' apron,
re-using the country cushion motif to great effect.*

Materials

As listed under Stencilling Basic Materials,
on page 10.

PAINT:
FolkArt Acrylic Colours: Blue Ribbon,
Bluegrass

OTHER MATERIALS:
Calico apron, FolkArt Textile Medium,
plastic-wrapped cardboard, plastic sheet,
stencil brushes, chalk pencil

Instructions

Before beginning, read general instructions
for Stencilling, on page 10.

1 Preparation
Wash the apron in a washing machine then
iron it to a smooth surface. Slip some small
pieces of plastic-wrapped cardboard into
the pockets to prevent any paint leaking
through onto the back. Also place some
protective plastic underneath the area
where you will be working.

2 Prepare stencils, following general
instructions on page 10. Refer to the pull-
out pattern sheet for actual diagrams.
Cut two stencils, one for the leaves and
one for the flowers. You will also need the
stencils from the Country Cushion project
(page 54).

3 Stencilling
Prepare the paint, one colour at a time as
described in the Country Cushion project.

4 Position the cushion stencil on the top of
the apron, then on the pockets, and apply
paint.

5 When the top and pockets are dry, locate
the centre on the hem of the apron and
mark this with the chalk pencil. This will
be the centre line for the larger stencil you
have just cut.

6 Measure the apron and determine even
spacing for the other two stencils which
will be applied. Use the chalk pencil to
mark the centre lines which will align with
the central registration marks of the stencil
sheet.

7 If the paint has dried, mix a fresh
quantity and apply it to the hem of the
apron as you have done previously.

8 Finishing
Again refer back to the Country Cushion,
and permanently set the paint by ironing.
Be sure to erase or brush off any chalk
lines, before ironing.

These diagrams show the combined stencil pattern. Refer to the pull-out pattern sheet for the actual diagrams to make stencils from.

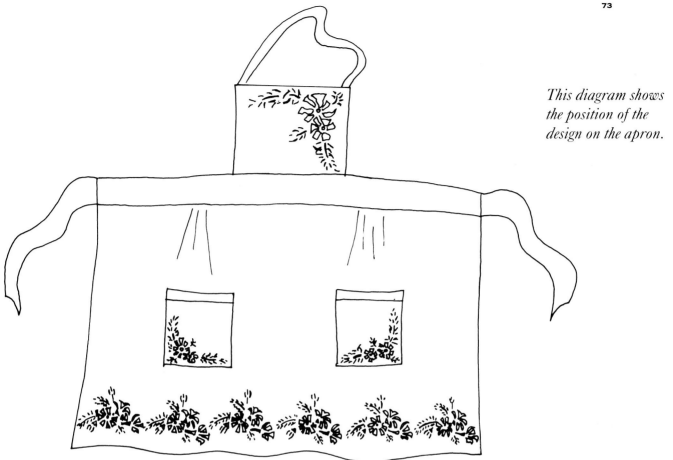

*This diagram shows
the position of the
design on the apron.*

*This is the reduced
version of the repeat
design used on the
bottom border of
the apron.*

Blue Bell Posy Tea Tray

Tiny Blue Bell Babies frolic on this romantically pretty tea tray.
The end result is worth the extra care you'll
need to take when cutting.

Materials

As listed under Découpage Basic
Materials, on page 8.
BASE COLOUR:
FolkArt Acrylic BaseCoat: Wicker White
PAINT:
French Wash Wall Wash: Sky Blue,
FolkArt Acrylic Colour: Blue Ribbon
OTHER MATERIALS:
Wooden tea tray, Simson paper featuring
Blue Bell Babies (no. SC505), sea sponge,
old raggy toothbrush, FolkArt Extender,
small bowl, sponge brush

Instructions

Before beginning, read general instructions
for Découpage, on page 8.

1 *Painted finish*
Sand the tray with fine sandpaper, paying
particular attention to the edges and
handles. Brush on 2 or 3 coats of Wicker
White BaseCoat with the sponge brush,
allowing the paint to dry and sanding
lightly between coats.

2 Shake the French Wash Wall Wash well
to mix the contents and pour a small
amount into a bowl. Moisten the sea
sponge, then dip it into the Wall Wash.
Squeeze out any excess. Drag the loaded
sponge across the tray leaving the blue in
soft lines. The sides and rim of the tray
also need to be dragged lightly.

3 Allow to dry, then spray with FolkArt All
Purpose Spray to protect the finish.

4 On your palette, mix Blue Ribbon with
Extender. Dip the raggy toothbrush into
this mixture and shake out excess paint.
Practise on paper before spattering the
tray. When you feel confident of your
control, draw your thumb across the
toothbrush so that the bristles flick the
paint onto the tray. Spatter lightly to add
interest to the finish of the tray.

5 *Découpage*
The design on the tray forms an oval, with
the Blue Bell Babies looking towards the
centre. If you wish to reproduce this
design you will need to look carefully at
the papers to match the elements used.
Since this paper has many fine pieces of
foliage to cut, good cutting skills are
required. However, because the
background is very pale, like the
background of the paper used, it is
possible to leave some thicker sections or
bridges in the cutting as these will later
merge with the background and not be
seen. If a darker background had been

used, very intricate cutting would have been required to remove all white.

6 Take particular care on this project to apply sufficient Mod Podge to the fine foliage so that it adheres properly. Also be careful, when smoothing it down with your fingers or a brayer, not to press so hard that little pieces are torn off.

7 *Varnishing and Finishing*

Special care is needed again when sanding. Use only the very finest grade or worn out wet and dry sandpaper, to avoid cutting through the glue layers.

8 Continue with the build-up of Mod Podge, then varnish, as outlined in general instructions (page 8). Finish by waxing and buffing to a deep soft glow.

This is a sample of the Simson paper used for the Blue Bell Posy Tea Tray.

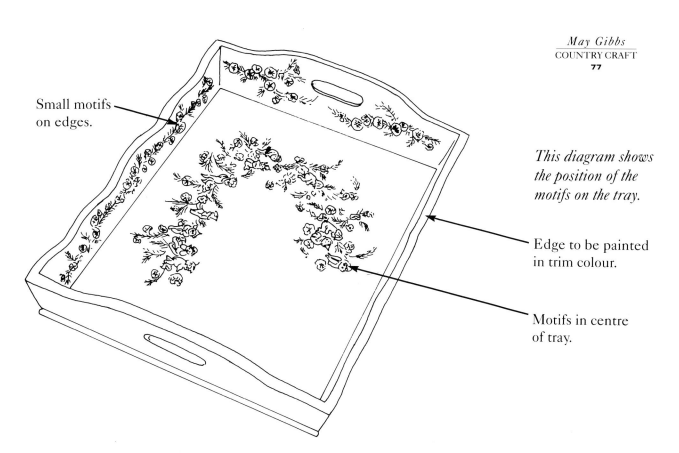

Small motifs
on edges.

*This diagram shows
the position of the
motifs on the tray.*

Edge to be painted
in trim colour.

Motifs in centre
of tray.

May Gibbs — naturalist, psychologist and artist explorer has mapped out a world of her own and conquered it completely.

ADELAIDE ADVERTISER 1918

Tales of Snugglepot and Cuddlepie was combined with its two sequels, *Little Ragged Blossom* and *Little Obelia*, in 1940. Since then the *Complete Adventures of Snugglepot and Cuddlepie* has never been out of print and the magic of the May Gibbs characters still enchants children and adults today. Harper Collins Publishers produce a range of beautiful children's books, stationery items and craft titles featuring the ever popular May Gibbs characters.

Complete Adventures of Snugglepot and Cuddlepie (H/B)

Complete Adventures of Snugglepot and Cuddlepie (P/B)

May Gibbs Alphabet Book

Alphabet Frieze

The Story of Little Obelia

The Story of Ragged Blossom

The Story of Snugglepot and Cuddlepie

Tiny Story of Snugglepot and Cuddlepie

Wattle Babies

Boronia Babies

Flannel Flower Babies

Gum Blossom Babies

Gumnut Babies

May Gibbs Address Book

May Gibbs Baby Book

May Gibbs Birthday Book

MAY GIBBS AND VICKY KITANOV

Ten Little Gumnuts

Ten Little Gumnuts Frieze

Ten Little Gumnuts Miniature

A Gumnut's Year